SLAYING THE DEVIL

One Man's Fight To Kick A Gambling Problem Into Touch

by

Mike Curtis

Bloomington, IN  Milton Keynes, UK

authorHOUSE®

AuthorHouse™
1663 Liberty Drive, Suite 200
Bloomington, IN 47403
www.authorhouse.com
Phone: 1-800-839-8640

AuthorHouse™ UK Ltd.
500 Avebury Boulevard
Central Milton Keynes, MK9 2BE
www.authorhouse.co.uk
Phone: 08001974150

First published by AuthorHouse 8/17/2007

ISBN: 978-1-4343-0324-0 (sc)

Printed in the United States of America
Bloomington, Indiana

This book is printed on acid-free paper.

INTRODUCTION:
A GAME OF CHANCE

They've just opened yet another casino in Manchester. It's another Grosvenor one. You know, that great big 'Leisure' enterprise who have casinos all over the country. I always used to prefer frequenting Grosvenor's gaming halls back in my gambling days, as opposed to those owned by Stanley Leisure, the rival player fighting for a large chunk of the gaming business in the area. Can't quite put my finger on why it is I preferred the former's establishments, I just *did*. Anyway, I'm not entirely sure if this new monstrosity can be classified as a 'super' casino, the type our wonderful government seems most keen to import from the grand old US of A. From the outside it appears 'super' enough, although, given the tone and in view of the whole point of this book, 'super' feels a most inappropriate way to describe this new place – I think I'll stick with 'monstrous'. Because that's the way I see such establishments these days.

The most distressing factor for me, though, is that it is situated a mere mile or so down the main road from where I, and many other trendy, cool, socially active young (ish) folk reside. Yes, that's right, it's bang in view on one of Manchester's strongest pulsating arteries that lead to the heart of the city, standing proudly and unashamedly for all journeying people to see, complete with typical gaudy neon lighting to tell all and sundry what kind of establishment it is. The location of this casino is certainly a new phenomenon as far as our town is concerned. The older established gaming joints are seedily tucked away in various crevices in and around the city – a haven for punters out of the way of the main areas in which many Mancunians tend to socialise. I see this kind of brazen, in-your-face attitude of the latest casinos endemic of the position the gambling industry has come to take in our day-to-day lives.

Whereas once upon a time serious gambling may have been viewed more as a pastime of certain strata of society, like the very wealthy with too much time on their hands, or undesirables wanting to risk their blood money, today's inexorable marketing and promotional machine ensures that *everybody* is targeted as a potential client/victim of some sort of gambling outlet. Whether it be horse/greyhound racing, casinos and their various offerings of gaming table, on-line 'Texas hold 'em' poker, sports betting right across the board from U.S. baseball to the Varsity boat race, political betting, the National Lottery, scratch cards and bingo. You could even throw in the stock market. I know personally of people who have lost fortunes dabbling in that.

I am the first to acknowledge that, on the face of it, a recreational punt of a fiver here or a tenner there on any game/sphere of chance is a relatively harmless activity, not exactly busting a gaping hole in the average man on the street's wallet. And many keep it to precisely that. But the truth is that by starting out with the odd, small bet of some form, the habit has the potential to snowball into a real, sometimes gruesome problem. Life is made up of a delicate balance, and I guess certain circumstances or personality traits can lead a person to do all manner of daft, reckless things. Compulsive gambling most certainly enters into this category. It can cut through every facet of a person's existence, affecting home life, job performance, leisure time and can even be personality changing.

This book is principally aimed at those who are experiencing, have experienced or feel that are susceptible to experiencing a gambling problem. Or for that matter those who are in denial that they occupy a place in those groups. How do you define a gambling problem? How do you recognize the symptoms? I believe that if gambling affects your life in any adverse way whatsoever, no matter how hard you try to dismiss this, there is a problem there; right through from the person who ruins his night out by losing twenty quid at the casino in the wee hours of the morning, to the person who loses his family, house and car by wagering hundreds at a time on the internet. I, personally, experienced a problem somewhere in between these two levels – I was gambling more than I could afford to, and certainly more than was good for my health and stress levels, but not to the point that it really affected others too badly. After something of a see-saw battle, I eventually triumphed. I am now 30 years old and am 'clean' once again.

When all is said and done, why put up with gambling in some way taking over your life, or worse still perhaps ruining it? I hope the experiences I go on to detail will make you ask yourself this question with even more vigour. You will see how I get drawn into all manner of gambling activity, how it spirals out of control and how I eventually come to realise that something has to be done about it. And I hope it dawns on you how only YOU yourself can extinguish the problem. Or, as the title of this book describes gambling as the 'devil', how only you have the power to ultimately massacre this beast. The devil of gambling is a strong force – and must be slain!

How The Devil Did I Get Into This?

It didn't start at the racecourse. It didn't start at a casino. It didn't even start with the odd game of cards at school, playing for a stack of pennies, five pences or maybe twenty pence pieces if the stakes were raised *really* high. If I recall correctly, these games were frowned upon heavily by the school authorities or may even have blatantly broken school rules, and took place mainly in the sixth form common room, usually involving only a relatively small posse of mischievous/bored adolescents.

Anyway, despite my growing affection at around this age (17-18) for anything even remotely rebellious, or even sometimes barely legal, I somehow never had the urge to muscle my way in to the lunchtime card games. Gambling simply had no pull on me whatsoever, especially since I was brought up with the notion that the bookies and casinos, of which there are many in my neck of the woods, were dull, smoke filled and positively damned places, frequented by ailing pensioners with yellow hair and teeth, ill-fitting, moth eaten old suits, dentures and little else to do with their remaining years on this planet other than fritter away their paltry state pension on anything that moved, or on the turn of a card. It was either their ilk, I was told, who filled these gambling joints, or undesirables of one sort or another. In short, it was fairly hammered into my impressionable young mind that gambling institutions were an absolute no-no and no-go! Hammered into me by parents, friends' parents, teachers and even by my oh so well reared school mates. Basically, I was raised by fantastic parents among decent people in a very decent middle-upper class suburban neighbourhood of Greater Manchester, surrounded mainly by professionals- the usual mix of lawyers, doctors, accountants, estate agents and even the odd stock broker. I went to a grammar school whose reputation precedes it, and which regularly churns out cricketers to serve Lancashire and even captain England (as in the case of Michael Atherton). No footballers, just cricketers. On the whole, the students of Manchester Grammar School were far too refined and gentlemanly to make it in the rough and tumble, shallow world of professional football. 'The game of the masses' is the idea with which we were imbued. 'Soccer' was played at school, but was certainly not encouraged to be taken as a potential career option. Cricket yes, football certainly not. So this gives you an idea of the kind of atmosphere I was raised in. quite prim and proper, really. And yes, there was a fair smattering of double-barrelled names among the 200-odd students that constituted our year.

So, I was well protected from the crude atmosphere of gambling establishments in my formative years, and indeed protected from any form of gambling at all, save those naughty little gatherings in the sixth form common room at lunchtimes, where buddies would assemble to attempt to pinch chicken feed off one another. Besides, I was far too busy with other distractions at the time- the usual stuff one is pre-occupied with at the stage of your life when hormones are zipping up and down your hyperactive, juvenile body. Yes, the fairer sex were actually appearing more and more fair in my eyes, as opposed to the unapproachable monsters I had up until then imagined them to be. And they were becoming more approachable for me by virtue of my rigorous exercise regime which had transformed my stick-insect like frame into one of a virile, athletic looking young colt (damn! I'm sure I had resolved never to talk about horses again!). And I was a keen sportsman- Sunday league football with my pals in the winter, and cricket in the summer. And, of course, I was well and truly pre-occupied with A-level revision during any other time which happened to be left over from this most hectic of schedules.

So, as I started out saying, I was an intelligent, athletic seventeen old with, as the saying goes, everything to play for, and even the occasional flutter had not crept into my almost perfect existence, as it was up until then. The world was a wonderful place; I was popular in several social circles and my appeal in respect of girls/young women was rising on the scale, if not absolutely spellbinding. I had never even set foot in a bookmakers or casino, and had certainly never entertained the thought of indulging in a day at the races. In fact, racing to me was merely that silly pantomime of a 'sport' that got in the way of cricket coverage on 'Grandstand', and when the latest results were read out they really did bore me, and any of my pals who happened to be watching T.V. with me, to streams of tears. As for the odds that were read out to accompany the names of the winning and placed horses, well, they may as well have been reading out advanced logarithms to me. 11-10 favourite? I thought this must have meant the aforementioned animal had won ten out of eleven races and was voted favourite looking horse at the at the race course that day! All in all, I didn't have the foggiest.

And I didn't *want* to have the foggiest clue as to how to enter a gambling den of any sort and get myself caught up in the hazardous pursuit/time wasting exercise of risking what funds I had against people who were more than happy to fleece any poor soul of their cash, and who would undoubtedly be more than adept at employing their shrewdness and experience in achieving this evil aim. I didn't want to get to a ripe old age to end up resembling one of these bedraggled, doleful old men who had spent the precious years of their life squandering small fortunes in the various offshoots of Britain's great gambling empire. And I didn't want to end up like my gran, who spent increasingly large chunks of her twilight years sat in a casino in Salford, apparently never leaving each time until she had "won back each and every penny" that she was down that night. And she really did make out that it was just a case of biding one's time in order to replenish any losses that had been incurred. Looking back, the untruth in that theory smacks you right between the eyeballs – if you have ever been a reckless gambler and chased your losses so damn hard you have ended up losing virtually everything you came with (and possibly more if you were silly enough to borrow more money off someone or other), you will know precisely what I am getting at. Point was, however, that in these prime throes of my late youth I did not, and had absolutely zero desire to, have any sort of inkling where this casino was or indeed where the nearest bookmakers was. Deep in my mindset, thanks to the (almost) flawless parenting skills of my dear mum and dad, not to say the stern and upright ethos of my school environment, was that gambling was for the unfortunate degenerates of society, or put more crudely, **losers**. Apart from my gran, G-d rest her soul, the only other individual I had encountered with any sort of inclination toward a punt was a close pal's uncle, and he was, by all accounts, kept a comfortable distance away from their family ranch. For my mate's mother was a very over-protective sort, and thought of her brother as a profoundly insidious influence on her kids. With the painful hindsight I have now acquired, maybe she wasn't being over-protective at all. Just plain sensible. One ought never underestimate the influence any single person has the potential to exert when they are part of your social environment, even more so when they are a close relative. I was always led to believe there was something wrong with this friend's uncle, as in that he was some sort of unfortunate case. No family is really complete without one! From the odd, fleeting glimpses I got of this character, he did indeed come across as somewhat odd, with regard to both his behaviour and appearance. His manner was nervous to the point of being almost apologetic, and his sackcloth clothing and flat cap took you back to the football terraces of the fifties. A bushy moustache verging on the handlebar variety completed the odd-ball look. I now know he was not backward or disadvantaged in any way. He had a nasty problem with respect to gambling. And as far as I know he still does.

Plans for my future were virtually set in stone. Although a rapidly maturing young fellow, I could still not yet offer a confident answer to THAT nagging question – 'So what do you want to be when you grow up, then?' I never had a ready response like most kids do in their childhood years, the kind of return of fire required to subdue the approaching snipers (made up mainly of interfering family acquaintances, as you can imagine!). One of my ostentatious, ruined childhood contemporaries had been proudly sounding out that he was going to be a 'Specialist' to anyone that would listen; I don't think he even knew what one was. I certainly didn't at the age of nine! By the time I was nearing the end of my oh so distinguished time at Manchester Grammar, I had come up with some vague, half-baked ideas that came in response to that damned, prying question, mainly relating to working in a field where I could use my half decent foreign language skills. Despite the vagueness surrounding what I actually wanted to do, I was supposed to go to a decent university, get a 2:1, get involved in a decent profession which would, according to my mum's wishes, mean wearing a pinstriped suit and sitting in a plush office in the posh bit of the city centre, and end up getting married off to childhood sweetheart Sarah. Strictly in that order. Well that was the plan, and up till then I was sort of happy to go along with it. My contemporaries at school were going to end up hard working, respectable pillars of their respective communities, so I was not to be an exception. Besides, if I wanted to fit in with Sarah's immaculately bred family, I was going to have to keep my nose clean and 'play the game'. And not the game I was about to embark upon!

ENTER THE DEVIL

My protective shell was soon shattered, however. Stuart was a strange sort, a kind of Boo Radley character who lived down the street from me. A gangly, skeletal figure who towered above my average sized frame at well over the six foot mark. To say he was strange would amount to a huge understatement. He carried around with him a security garment, a rag that resembled something between a decrepit old handkerchief and the remains of a shirt handed several generations down the family line. And yes, it stank to high heaven. I had never really bothered much with Stuart in my adolescence. He would occasionally, uninvited, invade our lawn, which doubled as the training ground for my not quite so exquisite soccer skills.

Whilst sniffing this insufferable excuse of a security rag, he would brag how he could swerve a football two directions in the course of one boot of the ball, a boast that generally ended up with the ball buried deep in the garden shrubberies and yours truly scrambling forth on hands and knees to retrieve it, often brandishing nasty grazes and nettle stings as a result. And it was all Stuart's fault. Anyway Stuart was very much a peripheral figure in those days. He was slightly older than myself, perhaps a year or two in it. I was quite contented with my existing gang, so it never occurred to me to go anywhere near his lot. Besides, we had little in common, really. He smoked, I hated the habit with a vengeance. He wasn't any good at football. I was busy winning Melchester Rovers 2nd X1 players' player of the year awards and the like. He believed in G-d. I didn't. He wore retro shirts and corduroy trousers. I wore Man U tops and 'trackie' bottoms. The list goes on - you get the gist. Stuart was a complete outsider (I really do wish I would stop using horse racing terminology) until one fateful day, the day Stuart wheedled his slimy way into our family fortress.

"Was just passing. Haven't seen you playing football in the garden for a while- so thought I would pop in to see you." Not the type to reject a neighbour's friendly advances, I let him in.

"So what are you up to then, in general?" I probed, well aware that the response would be non too enthusiastic considering he used to be spotted spending most of his school time loitering around the fairly expansive grounds of his house or even sometimes the streets. Or, as soon became quite apparent, the local bookies or casino.

"Am working at the fishmongers in Radcliffe. Come out stinking of fish, have to spend ages in the shower to get rid of the smell. Get a ton twenty a week. Just lost last weeks wages at the Albion (casino)."

He said this so matter-of-factly that I knew there and then what a loose cannon this guy was.

"You what?" I retorted, "you've worked your arse off in that stinking fish shop all week and have gone and flushed every penny of your pay down the loo just like that?!"

No verbal reply was forthcoming. A mere shrug of the shoulders was all he came up with. "What a head case", I mused to myself.

"Got a favour to ask," he then blurted, "Going to the lakes on Wednesday, and I need to win back some of that money. Got a tenner? Will pay you back when I get back on Friday. Promise."

"No. Sorry mate. No can do." I replied, remembering my mothers wise words: 'Neither a lender nor borrower be.'

Stuart sat there pensively, nervously sniffing that preposterous, stinking rag.

"Got another suggestion then."

"And what would that be?" I responded.

"Got a bank card? Switch or Delta or something?"

"Yep. Why you asking that?" I inquired, in suspicious tone needless to say.

"Well have you got ten or fifteen quid spare on your card?"

"Guess so."

"Let me have a bet on the dogs then. If you let me have a go with fifteen quid I'll split the winnings with you plus you get the fifteen back." He suggested this as though winning was a formality. . .

"Oh, go on then, we'll have a go. We'll get a few quid out of my account and see what happens. Where's the nearest bookies from here, anyway?" I inquired. I really was quite warming to the idea of having a quick flutter, especially since I had been getting more and more stressed about my upcoming A-levels. And I really had not done a great deal of revision, largely down to the fact that I had caught the romantic attentions of one of the finest fillies in our immediate neighbourhood. That plus the prospect of having to trawl through some completely turgid pieces of foreign literature which we had been set as part of our French and German A-level courses. So a trip with the mysterious Stuart from down the street to one of these seedy local establishments seemed like a great escape route to some short term stress relief.

"We ain't going to the bookies. And we're not even going to go and withdraw cash from your card at the hole-in-the-wall. We'll just bet on teletext."

"What d'ya mean, bet on teletext?" I asked, at this point completely mystified by the suggestion.

"Get channel four on, and go to page 601." Stuart's tone had become quite serious and business-like by this point.

At the same time I was, it's fair to say, flabbergasted that this lanky character, who to my mind led a life of, let's say, limited social interaction, knew that teletext even existed, let alone that he knew avenues through which this service could also serve as a live betting medium! It just seemed too easy; I could hardly wrap my head around the concept. You see, at this point of my earthly existence, there was no internet yet invading peoples' homes - having a computer at home was an exception rather than a norm - and common folk were yet to be seen walking the streets of our country twittering away about some sort of irrelevant twaddle on their mobile phones! There was the concept of the car phone, but to my mind these were confined to the possession of the filthy rich, such as my pal Simon's stinkingly rich entrepreneur of a dad, who was scion of a large family business empire, or your Richard Bransons and the like. So, to my mind, the possibility of having a bet on a hound or a horse from the comfort of my own living room was quite a bizarre thought, to say the least.

But Stuart knew all about it.

"You'll have to explain all this to me," I told him, as the betting market flashed up screen. He indeed explained carefully what the odds stood for, and even gave a brief discourse on how one could tell if money was going on a certain animal by its odds being shortened as the race time drew nearer. He was far, far sharper than I, with my misconceived preconceptions, would ever have given him credit for. Maybe, I ventured in my mind, I was in the company of a genius. He had muttered something in the past about being proficient at maths and chemistry, but claimed he was too lazy to do anything about it academically. Maybe he would channel his razor sharp mathematical mind in the direction of bashing these bookies. On teletext. Now. Stuart was certainly clued up on everything about punting by phone, and even had knowledge of some mysterious local call-charge number to listen to commentaries, instead of the preposterously expensive rates advertised on the teletext pages. We could therefore listen, on tenterhooks, as to how our fate would unfold, and I would soon know whether a smart little sum of money would appear in my paltry bank account.

And so Stuart and I got down to business, my ears all the while on high alert for any unexpected intrusion by parents. It was early afternoon, my mum was out playing golf and my dad was not due back until the usual time, around half five. But anything could happen, so I stayed on high alert.

"Traps three and four, the middle ones, are the ones to be on. They win most of the time," asserted Stuart. In my youthful naivety, I took this as read. We must have bet on around a dozen races, the first dog had won at decent odds from one of those favoured traps, and we had a tenner on it. Over thirty quid up, just like that. I had urged Stuart to stop at that, but he ruthlessly pursued his target.

"I need to get this up to a hundred quid, no less. Then I'll stop. Don't worry, you will get your fifteen quid back if we lose."

I was in no position to argue. This man's instincts were evidently supercharged, he just *knew* what to bet on and how much to stake. Yes, five or so bets were losing ones, but the winning ones, with their respectable prices, ensured we came out over two hundred and fifty pounds to the good. Stuart, with his ridiculously dated dress sense, plus pathetic security rag, had suddenly taken on a whole new image in my eyes; he was too intelligent to be bothered about being fashionably dressed. A man of his wit in the field of probability had no time for such mundane distractions. The look on his face was no longer dorkish. Instead it was a cunning look, the look of a man who knew exactly what he was doing. Meanwhile, my bank account was bulging with the winnings of his endeavours.

"The money goes into your account in two days time. I'll come round then at around the same time and we can pick it up from the cash machine."

So that was, basically, the pivotal moment in my life that I was introduced to the world of punting.

I excitedly ran the half mile or so to break the news of my magnificent win to Sarah, my first ever 'proper' girlfriend. She instructed me to immediately invest my new mini-fortune in some 'decent clobber'. I was expected to take her out sporting designer Armani jeans and poncey looking jacket. Apparently I had "crap dress sense", and anyway she "loved blokes with snazzy looking jackets." I was told where I could get one for around sixty quid, and she would even help me choose it. Kind girl. But I was all too happy to blow most of the winnings on these purchases. I could, after all, always win it back with my new mate Stuart. And he was going to take me as a guest of his to the casino one night, too, to enlighten yours truly further in the field of gambling. I didn't care that he had confessed to losing his weeks wages there several times recently, or that the same could potentially happen to me one day- I was just eager to sample an authentic gambling atmosphere, enjoy more winnings to keep up with my girlfriend's demands, and to continue and intensify my late-teen rebellion against the over protected and all too stuffy atmosphere that had encumbered most of my youth. The weirdo from down the street had come good. He had opened up a whole new world for my inexperienced eyes to behold. Dogs, horses, roulette wheels, blackjack, five-card stud poker, dice, football coupons, rugby, cricket- ANYTHING! I'd bet on ANYTHING. Bring it on. What a buzz. I was HOOKED. And thus far, it was all Stuart's fault.

DANCING WITH THE DEVIL
– THE EARLY YEARS

I was so hooked from this first, enthralling gambling initiation, that, as any as any real gambler with genuine gambling blood will testify, all I could look forward to was my next punt of one sort or another. You see by now, Stuart had, with very little persuasion necessary, broadened my foetal gambling knowledge to quite expansive proportions. Over those summer months we did the 'Full Monty', so to speak. Front that first buzz of winning on the dogs in front of the T.V. in my living room, the Grand Tour began. It was weird. To this day I still have no idea as to how Stuart himself had attained such vast knowledge of our area's gambling locations; from the local, decrepit Ladbrokes shop in Cheetham Hill, all the way to the swankiest casino in Manchester itself, called Tiberias, where the Manchester United manager Sir Alex Ferguson was reputed to be a regular visitor. How did this strange, gangly entity, who seemed a semi-recluse to me and my neighbourhood chums, have the intuition or sense of adventure to seek out all these places?

Before this gambling based friendship had kicked off in earnest, my encounters with Stuart had been sporadic. One of them, I recall, had occurred in the local park, which was literally just at the top of the road we both lived on. I was around 15 at the time, and was, typically, kicking around a football with some other local, over zealous Bryan Robson/Gazza wannabees. While we were kicking lumps out of each other and trying to emulate our childhood heroes, I remember spotting Stuart the wrong side of the iron railings by the lake, apparently closely examining something of profound interest to him. Sure enough, as twilight enveloped our imaginary Wembley and the rest of us wearily started to make our way out of the park, Stuart called out from by the lake.

"Mark, come here and see this!" even though it really was getting murky, and I was completely knackered and struggling with a wretched humidity induced thirst, I was too polite to tell him these facts and that I really couldn't be bothered with whatever discovery he had to show me. He unclasped his hands and there, in all its moist glory, was a small toad. He went on to proudly explain how a favourite pastime of his, particularly in damp conditions which were suitable for this, was to scour green areas for small creatures, frogs and toads being a favourite catch. This all confirmed in my then immature, narrow mind what a weirdo he really was. And not just to my mind; my equally cynical circle of spoiled-rotten mates thought the same. While we played footy and started experimenting with cheap cider on Saturday nights, Stuart apparently looked for frogs in parks and nature reserves! So with these memories to hand, my point was: How did this social outcast come to frequent virtually every gambling joint in the area? Who had introduced him to them? The answer would soon become quite clear, and these associates of his would lead me even further down the slippery slope of squandering more and more money at these bloodsucking establishments.

But for now, I had not ventured to ask how or through whose tutorship he had found his way into his dodgy recreational pursuit of gambling; I was far too excited to learn more. To learn more about which cards were the best or worst cards for the dealer in Blackjack; to learn more about the etiquette of playing last box (it really is *not* worth upsetting a table full of Chinese triads who have had a bad day and who are finding the cards going against them on the Blackjack table); to learn more about each-way trebles, forecasts, tri-casts and Yankees at the Bookmakers; to learn more about handicap betting in rugby matches; to learn more about filling out those complex looking football coupons and Irish Lotto slips.

And at the same time I was becoming ever less enthusiastic about my academic studies and University placement prospects. First to suffer was German Literature- I had already decided to do the bare minimum for this most dreaded of subject matters. By the time I was a regular, both day and night, at the Bookies and casinos, German Literature did not even exist as part of my a-Level curriculum! To hell with it, I thought. Not least because the particular novels we were assigned to make a study of contained strong anti-semitic overtones. Not very pleasant for a sensitive, young Jewish boy well aware of the atrocities of the Holocaust in 2nd World War Germany. French, the other language I had opted to study, came quite easily to me, so a minimal amount of revision would be required there. Then History. Ah! Dreaded History. We were supposed to read books as part of our revision schedule. And I *mean* books. Huge, fact filled monsters that dissected the battles of the English Civil War into the most miniscule of detail.

I didn't have time for this. Ok, Cromwell and his army of 'Roundheads' (or whatever they were called) had defeated James the1st. How, exactly, this came about was of no consequence to me (or to any other non-swats in our class of twelve, of which there were only four, myself included), and besides, there was far too much adventure to be had with the intrepid Stuart, and far too much placating of my highly judgemental, truly demanding girlfriend to be done. And sandwiched in between all this were the excellent cricket games in the park, which were played in the sweltering heat which was prevalent that summer (1995). Stuart was infiltrating my social life to a big extent now. Our common pursuit of watching six dogs scarper around a track at Monmore or Sheffield, or of anxiously waiting for the ball to drop on the roulette wheel, had naturally led him to become more a part of my general life. He even joined in our cricket matches, and his ability to smack the living daylight out of a cricket ball was quite astounding to me, given the evident lack of meat on his puny but substantial frame, and given that I had previously assumed his only skill was knowing where and how to trap toads to satiate his hunting desires. I was learning that my gambling Guru and mentor was something of a closed book – he really didn't let on at all about much. I was beginning to realise he wasn't the outcast, anti-social oddity I had foolishly presumed him to be. The fellow had a few strings to his bow. Several dodgy, tuneless strings maybe, but strings nevertheless.

I soon met his 'crew'. And what an experience this turned out to be. They were a motley crew of High School dropouts, dope smokers, binge drinkers, fraudsters, and, naturally, gamblers. The Chieftain of this small tribe was Geoff; a larger than life character whose physical frame was equally as large. He was dark and hairy and had a naturally brooding demeanour about him, he sported a seedy looking 'Goattee' beard and was rarely to be seen without a fag dangling out of his broad gob. He would often add a medallion style chain to the look, which would sit on his apishly hairy chest, exposed by a lack of buttons fastened on his shirt. This young man really did have a crazy streak – and whatever Geoff said, mostly went. And wherever Geoff decided he wanted to go, everyone usually went along with it. Having formed this friendship with Stuart, I was accepted without much argument into this posse of lunatics! I grew apart from the crowds I had up until then socialised with, the ones whose idea of late-teen rebellion consisted of stunts like staying out clubbing an hour or two later than they had told their parents, or even worse, missing a day out of their revision plans and having to cram in the missing work at a later date. I had gone along with this rather conformist lifestyle far too long now, and something far more enticing was lurking round the corner.

This new lot were an altogether more dangerous bunch, and it was certainly more a case of 'each man for himself' when we were out causing some sort of minor mischief. It was funny – the boy Stuart who lived but a few doors away from me had never given any clue of his association with these guys, who, it soon transpired, were ex-schoolmates of his and, according to all of them, were the most troublesome, havoc-wreaking bunch of hooligans their school had ever had to contend with!

They did pretty much accept me unequivocally as one of their own, possibly sensing I was not at all that enthralled with my steadier than steady upbringing and with the prospect of being chucked into the sausage factory that is University these days to study something I most probably wouldn't be that interested in. The only immediate drawback was Geoff's not so subtle interest in Sarah, my then girlfriend, and he even had the gall to mutter something about "having" her when she had "grown up a bit". But that was Geoff. He said **what** he liked, **when** he liked to **whomsoever** he liked. And he was far too big a bloke to answer back, really.

Geoff's bullish ways were, to me, only a small drawback though. His razor sharp sense of humour and sense of adventure more than made up for that, and just to be around the ridiculously dim-witted Jordan was an education in itself. And gambling constituted a major part of our activities. I could now see where Stuart had picked up the habit, and he had prepared me well for the gambling sorties we would so often go on. A very substantial chunk of my savings was eaten away at during the course of the next few summers, with the influence of my new found, roguish acquaintances a major contributory factor. Not only did we make all of Manchester's casinos a virtual second home, complete with the added convenience of free food and drink at some, but we would often sit there gambling away at the tables under the influence of one substance or another. That was playing with fire, really. It's hard enough to walk away from a table when things have gone distinctly pear shaped even with a clear head, but after an afternoon's recreational drinking with this bunch of Headbangers, it was naturally even harder to see sense and limit your losses. Just the kind of fodder the casinos undoubtedly welcome with wide open arms. Silly, jumped-up, cocky, drunk/stoned youths with nothing better to do with their time than fritter away savings/wages/ill-begotten gains at these dingy cess pits. On top of that, many a confrontation would rear up between any number of us over the tender subject of money, made all the more tender as a result of it having been swallowed up by the giant, greedy mouth of the gambling Beast. We must have blown thousands between us. Rows broke out over money lent and not paid back, more often than not because that borrowed money had not had the desired effect of clawing back the unhealthy deficit of a bad night's game of blackjack. It just meant that the debtor was going to be even more reluctant to pay back the loan on time, if at all in some cases. The worst was Geoff. He would use both his sizeable frame and his overbearing personality to bully anyone who happened to be around him into lending him money. And I do mean *anyone*, not just those in his immediate circle of mates.

On one occasion we found ourselves at a casino slap bang in the middle of Manchester's Chinatown, one of Geoff's favourites; not least because the atmosphere in there, especially at nights, was usually manically charged with the ranting/ squeals of delight of minute Chinese people as their bets either came good or ended up back in the croupier's chips dispenser. Needless to say, Geoff had taken great care to ingratiate himself to the regulars in there, and he was forever charming his way into the ladies' good books so he could nag them for a few quid when, more often than not, he had 'done his money' (i.e. lost again). If I was still a betting man, I would like to wager a fair few shillings that there are folk frequenting any of Manchester's casinos still waiting for that £50 that Geoff had blagged them to lend him all those years back.

And as for me, I was certainly not immune. As well as falling into the trap of spending increasing portions of my free time steadily bleeding to death the savings I was fortunate enough to have been endowed with, or to have saved up from the endeavours of various jobs over the years, these leeches for friends were also doing their bit to relieve this naïve young man (more like idiot, I would now hazard with the benefit of hindsight) of his funds. Whereas big Geoff would bully me with his breath close to my face into parting with my cash for the benefit of his gambling fund, Stuart, on several occasions, would make sick, empty promises about paying back any loan "in the next couple of days". This never materialised. I would almost always be waiting weeks on end for reimbursement, all the while listening to pathetic excuses as to why he hadn't paid me back on time. That was if I could get hold of him in the first place. This guy, whom I had previously considered to be some sort of gormless freak, was proving to be a most slippery and wily customer. Naturally, it has to be understood that it was the gambling that was the root cause of all these shenanigans, but in my book that was still scant cause to sell your so called mates a string of bare faced lies and false promises.

In the meantime, this vicious cycle of regular gambling, combined with alcohol and drug abuse (very often employed as a means of eradicating the memory of yet another hefty loss), was costing me dear in my general life development. Sarah had long gone, and although this silly new passion for punting may have been partly to blame, she was not exactly the benevolent type of damsel who would have stood by a vulnerable bloke going through any sort of personal difficulty. So, looking back, this was no great loss; she was clearly not my type, and I evidently I wasn't hers either. At the time though, I was completely distraught. Matters were made worse by virtue of the fact that Sarah lived, literally, up the road, and hence regular sightings of her proudly displaying her latest conquest, a dark, brooding veritable hunk of a masculine specimen, were quite difficult to avoid. By some minor miracle I still managed to string together an 'A' and two 'B's at A-Level that summer, but the damage had already been done, really. I was, at this point, a very hurt, angry young man, and what's more, I had fallen into the company of a delinquent group of youths whose whole existence seemed to centre around every vice known to man (one of them even resorted to the use of horse tranquillisers when he decided his marijuana habit was not getting him sufficiently 'wrecked' anymore).

All in all, this series of circumstances had really set me off on a dangerous and self-destructive path. I was persuaded to give university a go – for some bizarre reason I opted to study Economics even though the only areas for which I had had shown any aptitude at all at school were on the Arts side. So, of course, this little experiment didn't last long. I dropped out after about 3 months, which was also to prove a consistent period of time I would be able to stick future jobs, and during that process I managed to squander both my student loan, which amounted to around £1800, plus a bank overdraft of £800 in the local casinos and bookies. Well, the vast majority of it was. The rest was invested in cheap lager and the dodgy 'draw' that was regularly delivered to the student house I was now residing at. My woes were exacerbated by my loud, cocky housemate, a Londoner whose mega-wealthy dad owned the place. Because it was 'his house', his other four poor tenants were often treated with considerable disdain. On top of this, though, this young man had the gall to start seeing my ex, Sarah, right under my very nose; well aware of the fact he was causing yours truly great emotional distress by doing this. For me, ever the sensitive type, it was all too much to bear. I did soon move back to the comparative safety of the family home, but I was hell bent on hell-raising for the next few years; gone was the stiflingly rigid regime that was the course of study at Manchester Grammar School. I had done my time. And gone was Sarah, who had lodged a stake through my heart. I was going to go on the rampage. I was in with the right bunch of hoodlums anyway, and I was going to have a scream. I took on odd jobs in my early twenties to get me by- I worked at the local grocers for a time, did deliveries for a butcher's shop, worked in a JJB sports shop the other side of town, and even had a doomed trial period at an accountancy practice (I tried that one out because my uncle is a successful one). Living back at home, I had plenty of spare cash floating about. Cash to blow, of course. The trips to the dog track at Belle Vue continued to be a regular theme, as did the continuous tour of the half dozen or so casinos around Manchester. Many a night ended at chuck-out time, with most of us usually by that time desperately trying to claw back the wages we had so recklessly presented to the Grosvenor or Stanley Leisure organisations who shared Manchester's casino territory between them. Many systems, whether playing card games or 'the wheel', were tried, and many, actually all, failed. But no-one seemed to care. This was the mentality endemic among my circle of havoc-wreaking pals. Many a time we would make silly, desperate attempts to regain losses. After consistently playing the minimum £2 bet per hand all evening, I would often end up lumping on sums I couldn't really afford on the very last spins of the roulette wheel before closing time. This would often involve dashing out of the building to find the nearest cash machine (they weren't actually *inside* casinos at the time) to make panic-ridden withdrawals to fund a last gasp effort to emerge in a winning, or at least level, position.

Sometimes such tactics would pay off, but more often than not it was more of a case of staging one last stand and going out with all guns, and my temper, blazing. As all punters will admit, if pushed sufficiently, there is no worse pig-sick feeling than walking out of those doors nursing a hefty loss, a loss that often creeps up almost unnoticed as one is drawn into the dangerous routine of lapsing into a numb, neutral mindset as your tower of chips slowly disintegrates into a small heap of rubble as the night progresses.

So there we have it. In a nutshell, this is the course of events that took me from conscientious, clean cut sixth-former to the reckless, irresponsible youth I developed into in my early twenties. I had learned how to dance with the devil – and my most regular dances were those with the devil's own spawn that are the demons of gambling. As Sinatra used to sing though, the best was yet to come. . or more like the very worst in all reality.

DANCING WITH THE DEVIL
– THE LATTER YEARS

In the course of all this mayhem that had enveloped my once relatively clean-cut existence, there was something of a lull when it came to the impulsive, compulsive gambling streak that had more or less become an actual part of my persona. This would have occurred at around the age of 22, a year which would actually prove pivotal in the evolution of my already erratic character traits. By this time, I had successfully dropped out of University yet again (the third time, I think) and had accrued even more debts from that over generous 'Student Loans Company' and the ever-willing banks with their overdraft offers aimed at students. But at least these dubiously acquired funds were being put to good use now, instead of being frittered away in the gambling institutions of Cheetham Hill, Salford, Manchester and wherever Stuart, I and our merry band happened to find ourselves (I can recall one time we all 'did' our holiday money, in a drunken stupor, at the on-board casino on the ferry to Holland – Adam, the sugar daddy of our bunch, bailed us all out with generous loans!).

When I claim I was now putting whatever funds I had available to "good use", this is meant in only a relative context – Ladbrokes' loss was Witherspoons' gain; Stanley leisure's loss was Discotheque Royale's gain; Belle Vue dog track's loss was to the benefit of whichever girls were hanging around our crowd at the time. It was as if we had made a unanimous decision to incorporate more action and less dissipation into our free time. We partied increasingly, rooted out more of Manchester's famously eclectic clubs and took an increasing number of local, wide-eyed chicks (usually no older than eighteen) along with us for the ride on our journey of self-indulgence. It was one of these females who came to dig her claws into me. She was five or six years my junior, and in behavioural terms showed very little tendency to live up to her initial promise of bridging the age gap with an effort to act like a girl closer to *my* age. I was equally to blame for getting involved with her in the first place, interpreting my pals' warning about her apparent "psychotic streak" as jealousy on their part and not as a genuine message that I ought really steer clear. Well anyway, we can see where this is going – the whole thing turned out to be a disaster. This not being a romantic novel, I won't go into the sordid details of the whole affair. Suffice to say that I had got in too deep, and it turned out there was something about this girl and this relationship that really seemed to cut through the fabric of my being. Put it this way – by the time she had gruesomely chewed me up and ruthlessly spat me out, I was not a happy chappy. In fact, most of the ensuing six months were spent in solitary confinement in the attic at home, ruing not only the fact that my luck with women was turning out to be as bad as my luck with punting (the only certain thing about punting is that you *will* suffer more bad luck than good), but also that I had let myself get taken for a ride by this childish, head case of a female specimen. This all coincided with my second crack at accountancy coming to an abrupt end – something I had only pursued because it was perceived to be a 'safe option' and because my dad had been a successful one for over thirty years. I had been described by a senior partner at the practice, to my face at an appraisal, as "hopelessly unsuited to the profession", something I enthusiastically went along with as I had absolutely detested, in the strongest possible terms, my three month trial period of figure-tinkering. All in all, things were looking a wee bit bleak.

Things were quiet for the next couple of years. Everything – Higher Education opportunities squandered, jobs squandered, women and money squandered, the riotous partying, crazy and ill-fated adventures abroad, alcohol/drug fuelled family disputes – had seemed to get to me and bog me down somewhat. I needed a break. But this was merely the quiet before the fiercest storm yet, epitomised by my most reckless abuse of money to date as a result of a newly and overly charged gambling spree.

I had managed to revitalise my subdued spirit sufficiently to get back into some sort of working routine again, once again doing a delivery round for the local butcher, and had the good fortune to acquire for myself a cute, petite blonde girlfriend despite my growing cynicism and distrust toward the opposite sex. Both these minor triumphs were short-lived, however. The repetitious and sometimes physically arduous nature of the delivery job was too much to bear, and the latest girl in my life had turned out to be crazier and even more manipulative than the ones before. Before I knew it, I was back 'home', so to speak; back to doing what I did best when feeling I was under the cosh again.

Stuart was, believe it or not, married by now and had got himself a mortgage and kid to boot. That very day that I had told the butcher where to stick his chops and his delivery job, I was knocking on Stuart's door to find him, to no particular surprise, slumped on a settee that looked like it had seen decidedly better days. He had managed to find himself a wife from fairly wealthy stock, and she was a qualified teacher, too. This was of no inconvenience to him whatsoever, as it meant he could continue to practise his favourite pastime of shirking work, watching daytime T.V. . . . and punting from the convenience of his lounge. As I entered, muttering something about all that time and energy wasted at that wretched job at the butchers, Stuart had that familiar, knowing expression written on his face, which he wore every time I started harping on about my latest spectacular under-achievement of some sort.

"What you need is a nice cold can of Carling and a leisurely punt, you do," he opined in that familiar tone of his, the one which suggested he had the antidote for anything and that he generally knew what was best for you in any situation. "You need to get rid of that latest nutter of a bird as well," he threw in for good measure. I was actually not even going to argue, as I considered him to be quite close to the target on all scores.

In any event, after a brief catch-up about everything and nothing (I probably hadn't seen the guy for six months), we were no sooner supping early afternoon lagers, smoking Lambert & Butler cigarettes and sat in front of teletext with the betting market for the afternoon's first race up on screen, with the Daily Star form guide spread-eagled in front of us on the carpet. This was actually a significant first for me. In previous times, I had randomly and ignorantly picked out horses at the bookies on the odd occasions I did bother actually backing them, usually preferring to go for the fast and furious greyhound races. The horses, up 'til then, had never held any serious appeal to me. But that afternoon at Stuart's, I actually gave the form guide a cursory glance. Not understanding all the various stats that appeared around the horses' names, I noticed the suggestions of the two principle tipsters, Tony Lewis and 'Starform', and that in some races their tips were for the same horse.

"You see this, Stu, these tipsters both reckon Sharp Hat will win the 2.20. You reckon there's anything to be said for it?"

"Dunno," replied Stuart, in his typical non-committal manner and with trademark shrug of his bony shoulders. "Well I'm gonna go for it," I ventured, without giving even the scantest thought of maybe giving my latest crazy idea a trial run before plunging right in and lumping dough on it. I was still so ignorant about the horses that I recall going each way on an even money shot come my first bet that afternoon. I think I put £40 on the bet, and Stu (as I had been accustomed to calling him by then) and I went through the familiar routine of punting from home. We called up William Hills and quoted *my* account number; Stuart, as per usual, had nothing in his account available to risk.

"£20 each way on Sharp Hat please in the 2.20 at Catterick," I requested nonchalantly. The guy taking the bet asked, in an almost apologetic tone, whether I was quite sure I wanted to place an each-way bet on an even money shot. I conferred with Stuart.

"What's the problem with going each way on this horse?"

"There's just no point. Back it flat," replied Stuart, in a vein attempt to instil some sense into my decision. Me being obstinate old me, I shrugged off his counsel.

"Sorry 'bout that mate, just talking to my mate there. Yeah it's fine, stick it on each way," I affirmed. Stuart smiled and shook his head, as if to insinuate that I was in one of those moods where I wouldn't so much as budge out of the path of a bull gleefully hurtling towards the direction of his local china shop. That's to say I was not to be persuaded one way or the other. He was spot on. I was in a weird place, mentally, at that time of my life. In the grand scheme of things, I still wasn't a totally washed up, good for nothing failure, as society likes to label some people. But in the context of my immediate social environment people were beginning to talk – family, neighbours, ex-school-mates, even ex-girlfriends and their toxic-tongued pals. People talk – and invariably, the content always seems to get back to you by hook or by crook. Words to the effect of "What the hell is going on with Mike Curtis these days?" were being bandied about; "he drops out of this, he drops out of that; what's his problem? Hasn't he got any ambition?" With all this going on, I had reached a stage where I really didn't care all that much – so whether to back a horse each-way or on the nose at Stuart's house that afternoon, just after having acrimoniously walked out on another job, did not really amount to much significance. This was my mindset. Anyway, the damn horse won – easily at that. We went through the three meetings' cards that afternoon using my most simplistic method to back the horses, and I came out £140 to the good. Stuart, playing with money from my account, came out with around half of that, since I only lent him small amounts to stake given his less than reliable form for reimbursing his creditors on time. I was ecstatic.

" Look at that Stu, £140 for a couple of hours graft sat in front of teletext backing horses tipped in 'The Star'! That's pretty ok by my standards – I reckon we're on to something here."

We celebrated with another can of Carling and a spliff (marijuana cigarette).

" Don't get your hopes up too high – it *is* more than possible to lose as well," warned Stuart.

"Yeah, yeah, of course, I know that. But I reckon that if I stick to this method for a while, I'll come out with a profit of sorts."

"If that's what you think, then fine, go for it," he answered, never the type to put anyone, particularly myself, off having a good old streak of punting.

I had scraped together a few quid from heaven knows where the last few weeks, and was 'slumming it' in a £55 a week bed-sit a mere five minute walk from the family home. Needless to say, this abode very quickly became as messy as my mind. Then again, I'm a bloke. And blokes don't clean, unless they need some floor space to accommodate the playstation and whatever selection of rowdy rogues were round to challenge my impeccable 'Fifa '98' skills. Anyway, this doss house was to become my office. Forget the job hunt. I would be rising at the more than civil hour of eleven o'clock to stroll down to the newsagents for my pint of milk, deck of twenty Benson & Hedges and my copy of 'The Star', containing the astute advice of my new mate Tony Lewis and the accompanying 'Starform' suggestions. Then it would be straight back to the flat to peruse the racing pages and see which races had the main tipsters in mutual agreement. I didn't care about the prices, the size of the field, or about any of the stats which I would, in the future, be studying as if they were part of the Holy Bible itself. As long as Tony Lewis and 'Starform' tipped the same animal, I was bang there.

It was summer, so the racing would not typically get under way until after 2 p.m. This left me with an eager wait, time usually filled in with a leisurely fry-up and a couple of cups of tea (with 4 sugars to boost my energy levels, which were often flagging after copious excesses the night prior). Once set up for the day, and with the first viable race for my punting technique imminent, on went teletext pages 674/5/6 (the ones on BBC which show the betting market for each meeting) and the fun would begin. Naturally, each race punted on was listened to on the cheap, dodgy commentary line discovered by Stuart all those years ago. Back then, though, I was backing dogs a fiver a time, usually those in the middle traps, following Stuart's sagely advice which was taken as Gospel as far as my naïve, young mind was concerned. This time round, I had my *own* method, not backing hounds chasing a toy hare round a dingy looking dog track, but backing those magnificent creatures that are horses, mounted by those fine, talented sportsmen that are professional jockeys. And backing them with *proper* stake money. Surely, this time round, I was going to initiate a grand, profitable punting streak. It started well. I kept 'accounts' of each week's activity – I was going to do this properly. The first week yielded a profit of over £300, the second a little less, just over £200. I was ecstatic. I would no longer have to fret about finding my way into something half respectable to appease those individuals, as well-meaning as they were interfering, and get them off my back! I could make up some half-baked bullshit about investing my money wisely – I was not daft or brave enough to tell anyone of, what *I* thought, was my exciting, yet rock solid, gambling venture- and have the gossip merchants saying something vaguely positive, along the lines of Mr. Mike Curtis having finally landed on his feet. I know one shouldn't really take peoples' comments *too* seriously, and certainly not take them to heart, but for some reason they did seem to get to me more often than not.

Meanwhile, as what you could describe as a natural course of action, my stakes were increasing, slowly but very surely. That despicable trait of greed was seeping into my persona, as I attempted to maximize any winnings and so, in the process, nullify the memory and the deficit of all those bizarre evenings spent with that 'crazy gang' in my late teens and early twenties. As any experienced gambler who is realistic about his past fortunes will let you know, it is uncanny how any increase in stake money so often seems to go hand in hand with thumping **losses,** usually executed in the most inhumane of fashions in the guise of horses being beaten a short-head having looked the winner all over a furlong from the finish.

Sure enough, in the ensuing weeks after my initial three week show of profit for each respective week, the stakes were raised to £40 each-way (therefore a total bet of £80) per race, and sure enough, the period of profitable punting came to a shuddering, abrupt halt. I was starting to panic about how I was going to pay my monthly rent and bills, which were only around £230, and my angst caused me to throw caution to the wind somewhat. I more or less abandoned the initially successful betting system, which included exercising a modicum of restraint to stop when over £50 up for the day. This indeed meant I committed the cardinal sin of not quitting when ahead several times, and the rampant depressive feelings which were part and parcel of being on the end of such silly acts of profligacy were to become an all too frequent feature of many an evening; and there is, in my book anyway, only one type of medicine to cure such ailments – booze, booze and more booze. Not of the fish-like gulping proportions of a George Best or an Oliver Reed, but enough to render my legs sufficiently wobbly to greatly inconvenience my mini-trek back from the local pub, which, incidentally, included a danger-fraught crossing of the wooded short-cut that knocked a good few minutes off the time it took to walk the more conventional route back. One false step when negotiating the steep incline at the top, which would bring you back to civilization again, would be enough to send anyone, not least if they are in a state of inebriation, tumbling down the steep descent on the left side of the climb into a non too welcoming bed of thorny plant life. A sting-filled end to a rotten, losing day was definitely something to be avoided.

A certain visitor had started to regularly frequent my pit of a residence. This particular individual was, let's say, of the shady variety. He sold dodgy, fake Cartier watches and such delectable goods at £45 a time, and his not so esteemed clientele included several employees who worked in the massage parlours of Manchester and its surrounding areas. Even before I had got to know him personally in the course of one drunken evening at the local, I had heard of him and his dodgy ventures. Let's just say his reputation proceeded him. 'Darky', as he was known, was only a couple of years my senior, but the slick manner in which he comported himself betrayed an appearance maybe five to ten years older. I had been warned by several acquaintances **NEVER** to lend Darky money, as he was not to be trusted. Darky didn't do girlfriends – he was happy to feed off whatever scraps came his way when it came to 'bird' hunting. Darky certainly didn't do nine to fives. You get the picture by now; the image is completed by a healthy appetite for. . a punt! The flames of my new found zeal for backing horses were fanned by the arrival of this character into my life. The local bookies, a mere ten minute dawdle from my flat, was Darkie's second home. In fact, he called it "The Office". I had not yet ventured as far as this shop in order to indulge in what had become my main gambling passion. But Darky's entrance into my life changed all that. He would buzz on at my place each weekday at around twelve, and, if I was back from my trip to the newsagent by then, would slump on the mini-sofa while flicking through 'The Sun', and have me serve him black coffee. No sugars. Darky never really mustered much of an appetite before tea-time, so I would usually be spared the task of putting together an impromptu 'brunch'. Stuart would also pop in on occasion to complete a threesome; a trio of dodgy looking, skiving young men all with a common interest/sickness – heavy punting.

"So, fancy anything today? "would habitually be Darky's first meaningful contribution of the day following the usual exchange of not-so-pleasantries. I say this because Darky and I had journeyed along frighteningly similar paths up 'til then in our lives – kind of rough, booby-trap laden ones, maybe. But nothing *too* terrible had happened to either of us. However, we had both never really settled into anything work-wise, and had both experienced relationships with various girls/women over the years whose behaviour had bordered on the psychotic! So although we had both somehow scraped along money-wise and had nothing awful to complain about in relation to what some people do have to go through, it was as if the years had caught up with us somewhat, and at the sober hour of high noon, did tend to sway toward the side of grumpiness, especially as either one or both of us were involved in a small battle to rid our systems of excesses incurred the previous night.

By actually dragging myself from my pit to the 'office', the term by which I had joined Darky in referring to the local Ladbrokes shop, a whole small new world was opened to me – well, not quite a world, but a kind of club, I would say. Yes, I had been in there several times over the years, mostly with Stuart, but was not at all part of the furniture there. My past gambling trips had taken me all over Manchester to various casinos and bookmakers, but I had yet to frequent any single place where I could be termed a 'regular'. All this was to change. You see, Darky had taken me under his wing, and I was to become a regular accomplice of his at 'The Office'. Through this new change in routine away from the comfort of betting from my cosy little bed-sit, I was alerted to the delights(!) of in-depth study of that 'Bible' of racing fans – The Racing Post. I had known of this publication previously, but the prospect of studiously scanning its analyses of the day's races had not yet appealed to me. I was happy with my simple little system using 'The Star'.

By going daily into the office, though, delving into the complexities of the Post's analyses became a must for me, especially as my system had short-circuited and I had reverted to considerably desperate measures to try to reverse my fortunes, coming up with various new tactics based on my daily study of 'Starform', such as backing a horse at 'decent' odds (i.e. 4-1 and upwards) as long as it was tipped by someone in this paper and as long as the field of runners wasn't too big. Again, no sort of examination or practical trial was given for this technique. I simply steamed in, £40 here, £80 there – right through the day's cards.

Now, I thought, I could really make some inroads. I had acquired a considerable sum on credit, including a £5000 bank loan, and a plethora of credit cards with introductory interest-free offers on balance transfers. And, believe you me, there were plenty of balances by then that needed a healthy 'hit' off these generous credit-card limits I'd been allotted. Or, more like, those that my dad had been allotted. I had accumulated several cards under *his* name due to his more favourable credit rating and resultant higher levels of credit that were offered to him.

With this financial ammunition available, I was ready to steam ahead and use my new super-ally 'The Racing Post' to make some inspired choices and back some big winners in the coming months. Just how deluded I was, was to be revealed in the tempestuous months thereafter. What a silly young man.

Run By The Devil

I had phone accounts with the major bookies – Ladbrokes, Hills and Bet 365. I didn't have any accounts on the internet – because I didn't *have* the internet available, being something of a technology-phobe. Not only that, but when would I actually have used it anyway? I was quite happy to conduct 'business' off my mobile phone, usually in the secure (and often whiffy) confines of the toilet in 'The Office'. After all, I didn't want the loitering Darkie, or 'The Shadow' as he had come to be referred to by many people because of his propensity to monitor your every move, eagle-eyed while often invading your space, to overhear what were by now the astronomical wagers I was laying over the phone. When he did probe as to how much I had lumped on any particular horse, I usually shrugged off his enquiry with a nonchalant reply like, "Nothing much, mate, only a score (£20) each way." The reality was that, by now, I was staking £200, on average, per bet. But I didn't want Darkie to get wind of this – he was never too shy to ask outright for a loan, so I didn't want him to discover either that I had access to fairly substantial sums of cash (albeit mostly on credit), or that I had managed a big win at any time, which would be another angle for him to come at to sniff about for cash. I would never begrudge lending money to a friend in need – which Darkie often was because of his quite dreadful money management skills. I would dread to think of the consequences if he were in charge of the National Treasury! I would never want to lend Darkie money. He still has, to this day, a string of creditors who had been duped into 'investing' into some dodgy scheme or other that he was involved in, or whom he had simply declined to pay back. So my betting habits and big wins were kept firmly under wraps.

And boy, did I have some big wins. Not the ostentatious type, I never 'shouted down the house' at the shop when my punted animal crossed the winning line first. A quiet, self-congratulatory/relieved clenching of the fist sufficed. Besides, I didn't want to incur the wrath of those unfortunate souls who had backed a loser. Especially big Scottish Dave – a fearsome looking individual; around 6'2", flame haired, broad and bulky as a rugger player and his image was topped off with a well pruned ginger moustache. He would not have looked out of place, complete with kilt, roaring at King Richard 1st's English army on the front line of William Wallace's assembled troops of vengeance-seeking Scottish savages. Darkie had informed me that Scottish Dave had a history of 'losing it' in this Ladbrokes shop. On one occasion, he was so peeved at losing a bet following a jockey's less than strenuous attempt to get his mount home first, that he threw a couple of handily positioned stools at the T.V. screens! He got barred for that, but he was back now. Anyway, this was not a man to be crossed. I got to know all the regulars in the shop – Greek Steve, old Basil and Harry (who, apparently, had been regulars for over thirty years) and the rest of the odd-balls and nut-cases who made up the usual crowd. One fellow who occasionally popped in was, reputedly a **huge** punter. He was only around thirty, and his home was, apparently, furnished with the latest big-screen plasma T.V.'s to watch the fate of his investments. There were constantly conflicting reports of this guy's progress, who was supposed to be of the status of professional punter. One minute, Miro, a Croatian guy who had got pally with Colin, would be animatedly enthusing about his latest bumper win.

"I tell you, Mikey, Colin had £5000 each way on this horse, Moonlit Harbour, and it won. It was 4-1! Lucky bastard."

Two weeks later, he would approach me again, and in his best, eastern European, broken English would regale me with the details of the man's latest horrendous blunder.

"Mikey, you heard about Colin? He put all his winnings from the last two weeks plus another £25000 on Rooster Booster in the Champion Hurdle. He's re-mortgaged his house again because of this!"

I gasped in amazement, I could not even begin to imagine how I would react if in Colin's shoes. The man had backed the much fancied Rooster Booster, albeit at the skinny price of 11-8, to win hurdling's showpiece race, to the tune of tens of thousands of pounds. It had got beaten, when looking a good bet to win a couple of furlongs from home, by the 33-1 Irish chance Hardy Eustace. How gutted must he have felt? I felt nauseous just contemplating how he might have felt after this upset.

"Colin doesn't give a sh*t though, he'll carry on. He's fearless," insisted Miro.

I couldn't buy that. How could any human being not care about such a substantial loss? *Of course* he cared. To lump such daft money on one horse, in the most competitive and hence most furiously quickly run hurdles race of the season, at the most demanding of tracks – Cheltenham – he must have had to admit to himself that he had a giant sized gambling problem.

Not that *I* was getting any better. My desperation to rake in decidedly large lumps of cash had led me to continue increasing my bets. I was soon doing £500 bets. Sometimes I would punt on a pretty short priced favourite that I fancied – usually as a result of The Post labelling a certain horse as being "the one to beat" in that particular race. This always caught my attention. Or sometimes I would go each-way on a second favourite, usually between the 3 and 5-1 mark. My wins – and, more significantly losses, had reached the three figure threshold. A couple of losers at £500 a piece, and there we go – I was in for a hefty loss. This would normally trigger a gut-wrenching reaction and a craving for alcohol – lots of it – to numb the pain!

There again, on the other hand, a big win would effect, naturally, emotions on the opposite end of the scale. Darkie and our local boozers would often benefit from a bender of riotous proportions off the back of a successful punt and subsequently a healthy bank/credit card balance. These wins, though, were tempered by some horrendous losses. You see, unless you have been there yourself, you don't realise how easily one can get sucked in to chase ones losses. And it is a vicious circle – let me explain. You don't want to walk out of the bookies with that sickening feeling that you have lost, that they have got the better of you. Or you will often regret backing a particular horse after maybe an hour of painstaking analysis in *The Post*. This game plays with your head – make no mistake about it.

There are absolutely no guarantees, and, quite frankly, you will find that there are so many better things to do with your time than suffer the stress of watching what you thought was a 'good thing' run like a pig with acute gastroenteritis. With a large patience threshold and an accompanying dose of rigid discipline, you have a good chance of limiting losses, or even showing a profit of sorts in the long run. But – and let me stress this a second time – **there are no guarantees.** Because the powers that be of the sport, the bookmakers, are out to get *to* you and ultimately to *get* you!! And trust me, they know how to do it, to a tee. They even employ psychologists to come up with the best ways to irritate their clientele and consequently have them hand over their money in pure frustration. This, it goes without saying, also applies to casinos. They stick you in an environment completely geared to wind you up, to fray your nerves. And it is all legal. For example, you will notice that casinos are dark places (I mean this in a physical as well as metaphorical sense). There is never any daylight because there aren't any windows. They do not have any clocks visible. Even the carpets and general design of the interior are designed to have a negative psychological effect. They create another world for whoever enters their premises. People, generally speaking are not that strong. They fall for the whole thing hook, line and sinker, and can end up blowing horrible amounts of money, amounts they would *never*, in a sane state of mind, in a normal environment, dream of losing. I've done it, you've probably done it, and countless others have done it. We may all go into the bookies or casino, or even a card game with mates, with a specific budget we are prepared to possibly lose that time; but the nature of the beast is that it rarely pans out like that.

I know that at the height of my fascination with betting on the horses, I could all too easily lose control. An ill-informed punt or a non-trying jockey would be all it took to 'set me off on one', so to speak. This dark mood, accentuated by what was supposed to be the consolation found in six pints of Carlsberg Export, would lead to even more rash decisions the next day. Your biggest wins will almost certainly be overshadowed by the colossal losses incurred by chasing your money – time and time again. Unless you are a multi-millionaire you will have to go through that awful process of regret and double regret about the reckless actions you have undertaken to swell the coffers of those blood-sucking leaches that are the bookmakers and the casinos. You will toy in your mind with ways to grab back some of what was once yours. I know people who have done all sorts with regard to this – card fraud, swindling accounts at work, thieving from or not paying back generous loans to family and friends. Even though Darkie will not admit to it, even when pushed after a few lager/whisky chasers, it is quite obvious he is involved in, let's say, underhand activities to finance his long standing addiction. Not only is it an addiction, a disease to him, but he *genuinely* pins his hopes on combination bets involving several long-odds horses or football teams in a vague, vain attempt to recoup some of his years of losses. Basically, he needs luck on the scale of a substantial Lottery win to pull that one off. But that is the sad way it has worked out.

I am a little more fortunate than, say, Darkie, as I have never gambled beyond my means i.e. gambled to the extent I was too skint to purchase the basic necessities to live or to fund one's usual leisure time activities. I have had a problem. A **big** problem, no doubt. I have blown horrible sums of cash, culminating in a £7500 loss in **one** day, thus wiping out the available funds on two credit cards – sick when you think about it. But I have never resorted to begging, borrowing or stealing (the three deadly sins for a skint gambler to commit) to finance my habit. I know of one local guy who has had to flee the country because so many creditors were chasing him up for money he had borrowed in order to keep gambling. It's all very sad. The world of gambling does seem to have this certain weird potency to lure in many an unsuspecting victim. I know a lot of people who get involved as a kind of escape from whatever other problems may be dogging their lives, or maybe just as a result of pure tedium. This has to stop though. Whatever the reason is for becoming entrapped in a gambling addiction, those that run the businesses that milk the masses of their hard earned money are responsible for a heck of a lot. You can always argue how man has free choice, certain responsibilities to watch his/ her own back etc, etc. This, however, cuts no ice with me. There is enough free choice in this world just simply getting by on a day-to-day basis, without these crooks tempting in those who are naïve and vulnerable enough to get involved in a serious way.

Other people might argue another couple of points; firstly, if you are going to criticise the presence of gambling institutions, there are no limits to the lengths you can go to in order to put certain activities in a bad light; why should a person walk into a pub? If you go for that first pint with your uncle Charlie as a fresh faced eighteen-year-old and acquire a taste for good ale, who's to say that, in time, you won't wind up a helpless alcoholic headed for the gutter before you know what's hit you?

Secondly, there are those who will argue that gambling is a great British tradition that has entertained men and women alike for centuries. Even the humble sandwich is named after a certain Earl of Sandwich, who, in his wisdom, found a way of putting together the contents of his snack between two pieces of bread so he could eat with one hand free to engage in his favourite pastime of playing cards! But just because something is traditional does not mean it is good. They say prostitution is the oldest profession known to man. Most fathers, though, would not wish their own daughters to end up in such a 'vocation'. Besides, if you were to conduct a survey, most people would, without a moment's hesitation, brand the practice abominable. Maybe gambling isn't viewed to be quite as morally outrageous as the aforementioned activity, but I, personally, would not shed a tear if gambling in its every form was deemed an unnecessary evil in this country and was banned completely.

It appears, though, that this current Labour government is of a completely opposing philosophy. They want to build "super casinos" in Britain's major cities, and have even spoken of plans to turn Blackpool, already replete with scores of gambling attractions (not to mention other social ills), into a mini Las Vegas. On-line gambling is booming, there is more racing than ever (even an all-year-round jumps season), and on Sky T.V. all you have to do is touch the 'red button' to bet. It's omni-present. And it is spreading like the plague.

GET THE DEVIL AWAY FROM ME

There comes a time in everyone's life when you start to question what the hell you're doing and why. It could concern absolutely anything - why you've been stuck in the same job for 25 years, going through those same boring motions again and again, hour after hour, day after day, year after year; why you've been stuck with the same wife/husband/partner for 25 years, even though any hint of mutual love and affection has long since disappeared; why you've lived in the same house for 25 years, even though it's packed to the rafters with all your demons that have accumulated during the inevitably bumpy ride that constitutes the journey that is life; why you're still playing golf after 25 years, even though your swing has gone to pot and your dodgy right knee keeps playing up by the time you reach the twelfth hole!

It's only natural to question; after all we are all human beings and human beings have a very natural and healthy propensity to question the whys and wherefores of their respective existences. The flip side of the coin to this particular reasoning is to present the very understandable theory that man is only truly happy when he is happy with the lot he has been allocated, and that one doesn't need the aggravation that comes with questioning the virtue and worth of every facet of his/her existence. But not only is this angle of thought an easy way out, it is also one that avoids the issues that could inherently improve the quality of an individual's life. After all, what's the use of rotting in the same cesspit of unnecessary and unwanted habits and situations, when all you have to do is strive a little to make some positive changes to your existence. All it takes is to be honest with yourself about whatever it is that deep down, even though you have shovelled layer upon layer of protective grit over it, troubles and eats away at you and prevents you from having that light-on-your-feet, worry free feeling.

I am not stating that anyone with a gambling problem, however long or short term, is bound by such pervasive feelings of anger, guilt, helplessness and doubtlessly countless others, depending on the person. But from a personal perspective, I certainly went through many years entrapped in the sphere of such negative emotions, which were accentuated as my gambling problem spiralled hopelessly out of control. I acknowledge that some people perpetually choose to turn a blind eye to their problem, or that others simply do not care two hoots, even though losing so much money may have led to catastrophic consequences in different areas of their lives. This surely is not the route to go down, though, and certainly not for those with responsibilities such as supporting a family, running a business or holding down any other position where other peoples' wellbeing or money is at stake. If you follow the news, you may recall the case in 2006 of a Halifax bank branch manager who developed a particularly rabid gambling streak, mostly for the horses. Including money shelled out for tipping services (which evidently didn't help very much), this particular man managed to run up losses amounting to over £7,000,000. Or, put more accurately, he succeeded in running up losses of these proportions on behalf of the Halifax branch itself; he wasn't even playing with his own money. By the time he had finished, he simply left an 'i.o.u.' for £7,000,000 in the bank's safe! But this guy's actions didn't just affect him – they affected his whole family, from whom he promptly fled once he came to the realisation that he had to face the music for his extravagantly naughty deeds. You see, this is the kind of case that really saddens me, as the man's gambling problem snowballed to the extent that he threw away what was once a very stable financial position in return for nothing but financial ruin. I don't know how things have turned out for him and his family, but it is hard to imagine that his losses have in any way been written off or that he has been given a reprieve by those authorities involved in investigating the enormous debt, even in view of the fact that this fellow obviously had an dose of gambler-itis of the highest intensity. Where he has winded up is anyone's guess, but, although I am the first to acknowledge that money and status isn't *everything* in life, most people would be non too thrilled at falling from the upper rungs of the societal ladder down into the abyss that is occupied by those who have thrown away virtually everything by succumbing to one wretched addiction or another.

I am one of the more fortunate ones. I gambled away a hell of a lot; wages, savings, student loans, bank loans, credit cards, and any other cash I came across one way or another. But, following on from the distinction I made before, my recklessness and irresponsibility only affected *me*, in the main. Yes, there were the nasty side effects of a bad day at the races or the casino like snapping viciously at those immediately surrounding me – girlfriends, parents, sisters and close mates. Or the bizarre, consolatory benders I would put myself through, often ending in unwarranted abuse and generally anti-social behaviour directed at who ever was unfortunate enough to cross my path that particular evening. But all in all, nothing too serious ever developed; no houses were repossessed, no businesses went to the dogs (pardon the pun), and no one was violently abused at any stage. You hear all sorts of (very disturbing) stories about folk afflicted with strains of the gambling scourge. Several times a year, I read or hear of a local bookies being held up for cash, or, more recently, even ram-raided by night. Nothing would surprise me less if it transpired that some of these robberies were perpetrated by people who had lost far more than they could afford to at these shops (effectively robbed by *them!*), and were exacting some sort of desperate, fiscal revenge.

That is, quite frankly, how I see it. Bookmakers operate a daily operation of daylight robbery! How they can sleep at night, knowing that their whole *raison d'etre* is to squeeze as much as they possibly can, using whatever tactics are to hand, out of the general public is quite beyond me. Even at the height of my profligacy, I often had it in my head that however much I had 'done in' that day/week/month, I could never in a million years sleep with an easy conscience had I been the one on the other end of the court who was dishing out the deadly combination of shots that was reducing my opponent to rubble. Or in this case, the bookie/casino owners who are happy to ruin however many lives. Yes, yes, yes. I know there will be those who argue the whole 'free choice' aspect of this particular debate, that no one exactly drags anyone kicking and screaming into a gambling atmosphere, and that those who want to gamble should be entitled to do so. But ask yourself: is it all really worth it?? Gambling ruins lives, families. Whatever angle you look at it from, this is the **reality.** Casinos know it, bookies know it, and everyone in any way involved in gambling knows it.

We all have responsibilities and choices, but personally, I lay the blame squarely at the feet of those who have instigated and control the gargantuan gambling industry.

But how is this ever going to help the tens of thousands caught in the ravages of the current gambling epidemic? The truth is that it isn't going to help much – although, I reckon you *can* use this anger against the gambling hierarchy in pursuit of a positive outcome. If, like me, you have lost a fortune over the years which has had a direct effect on your financial position, not to mention all the precious time wasted in the actual act of losing all this money and the false hopes harboured of somehow winning it back, there should be little difficulty involved in arousing some particularly strong feelings to ensure you do something constructive about the problem. Here are some of the things that went through my head as I reasoned with myself as to why I should kick it all in:

A) Wagering all this money I can barely afford to simply doesn't feel right. There are so many better things I could be spending it on, or I could even start putting it towards savings of one sort or another.

B) Why should I put myself through those infuriating range of emotions which ensue after a heavy loss or a generally bad day at the races, or for that matter the false sense of ecstasy which usually follows a large win?

C) There are much more pleasant and interesting places to spend my free time rather than a bookies, a casino, or even a racecourse or dog track. Why spend time around people with agitated, or even aggressive expressions on their faces because of the bare faced fact that they are gambling more than they should be.

D) Why should I have any part in lending support to an 'industry' that makes no bones about the fact that its primary objective is to commit daylight robbery on the masses by whatever methods or technology is available to them. It is, in my view, a ritual form of humiliation to voluntarily hand over large sums of cash to people who give you the stingiest chances of winning. Trust me, when a bookmaker compiles odds for a forthcoming event, they will reckon on a price that represents less value than it should justly be, and then cut it some more, just to cover their own backs some more!

E) I could be improving my golf swing instead.

If you, yourself, are sufficiently determined to get out of a voracious punting habit, I am sure you will come up with more reasons as to why it would be of great benefit to quit. And I reckon that it *is* very important to come up with specific reasoning as to why it makes sense to stop. After all, the gambling industry uses any amount of psychological ploys and advertising to try to get the public to take part. Therefore it only makes sense to battle back with your own determined and well thought out reasoning to stop you from taking the bait.

Let's take a practical example. You are walking past your local betting shop on the day of a big football match, and the match odds are emblazoned in spectacular multi-colour all over the shop window – Manchester United 15/8 Chelsea 11/8 Draw 9/5. You might well get it into your head that one of these prices represents good value; maybe United have hit a streak of very good form and look a decent bet to 'do' Chelsea, especially with home advantage. Maybe the next person might fancy backing the draw, believing, quite reasonably, that these two very good sides will cancel each other out. Forget it. There is **no** value to be had. A fairer reflection of the match odds would probably read – Manchester United 11/4 Chelsea 2/1 Draw 3/1. But the bookies aren't in it to be 'fair'.

My advice is as follows; don't even give the betting shop window a cursory glance in the first place – simply walk on as if it weren't there (if only Adam had undertaken the same attitude towards those apples in the Garden of Eden!). Buy yourself a few lagers at the off-licence a few doors further on, and resolve that you are going to invite a couple of mates round (non-gambling ones of course) and enjoy the big game without the twangs of angst which accompany the lumping a good slice of your salary on it. And, of course, turn a defiant deaf ear to any promptings through the t.v. to place a bet from the comfort of your sofa. Your sofa doesn't feel so comfortable after a dubious last minute penalty robs you of a fair few quid that could have come in handy for the weekend plans.

One thing to bear in mind is that – and I repeat, having pointed this out earlier- this book is aimed specifically at those who have come to feel that there is a gambling problem deeply ingrained in their make-up; that this problem has taken some sort of hold over them, is affecting their lives in any manner of negative way and that they feel they don't quite know how to get out of what has become a vicious cycle. A cycle of gambling compulsively, having to go through all those problematic consequences that arise as a *direct* result of the 'sickness' (and *yes!* Although you might be loathe to face up to this, compulsive gambling **is** a sickness), but still not quite having the right medicine to hand to cure the ailment. I am certainly not going to be so arrogant to claim that, just because I have slain my own personal demons, I do have some miracle cure for any and every individual's gambling disease, because first up, everybody is so wonderfully different in nature from the next person, and one person's plan of attack to defeat the gambling enemy that has so to speak invaded them may well prove a quite ineffective course of action for someone else. Plus – and I really am at pains to point this out in the strongest possible terms – there *is* no magic 'cure'; it's not like there is some sort of anti-biotic available out there like, say, the equivalent of the penicillin one would take to rid themselves of a throat infection. It is absolutely a case of summoning up sufficient guts and determination to completely wipe out the habit from your day-to-day routine. Because that's, unfortunately, what it does. It creeps, or perhaps in some cases storms in, to your very routine that constitutes your **life**, like a well-oiled, ruthless military machine that invades another unsuspecting, vulnerable country. You could even compare it to Germany invading Poland, I suppose. Because that is the extent of the insidious, potentially all-conquering evil that so many people in the developed, so called 'civilised' world are so cruelly exposed to.

I haven't yet really mentioned the routinely accepted various channels of help for those that do realise they have got a problem and decide they want to do something about it, such as seeking counselling or attending GA (gamblers anonymous) meetings. Personally I would say yes, give these channels a go if you feel comfortable with the idea and you feel as though they could genuinely help you with your struggle. As it happens, I have personally never felt comfortable with the idea of discussing out my problems, of whatever nature they may have been at various points in my life, with a stranger or, that said, a whole bunch of strangers going through the same thing. I have always been more at home with the idea of using close friends and family (poor cretins) as an emotional punchbag, or for seeking out ideas that may help combat whatever it was that was bothering me at any given time. But whichever route you choose to take to help yourself, that is precisely what it does boil down to – **helping yourself.** With all the good will in the world, no amount of outside influence can actually do your job for you. You have to be strong enough in *yourself.* How am I so sure of this?

Because I have heard of more than enough cases of people attending GA or the like for *years and years*. And they still suffer the same old, bastard of a problem. Enough said.

THE SLOW SLAYING OF THE DEVIL

I can explicitly recall the various feelings and internal arguments that started to nag away at me, which meant I was, at last, ready to commit to the immense struggle that would be my painstaking hike up the colossal mountain at the top of which was the clear, pure air that would be the reward for being free of this ghastly addiction, and breathtaking views of all the beautiful surrounding areas that would be mine to behold once I had struggled over the gruelling, rugged terrain that represented all the horrible problems my horrid addiction had afflicted me with.

As you can clearly tell, I am no bloody Wordsworth when it comes to my attempts at painting a colourful picture of the travails I undertook to smash my problem into smithereens. But you get my drift. As any true addict of anything will testify, kicking the whole damn thing into touch – for good – is a personal struggle that equates to a truly huge, mountainous struggle. And the trek up the mountain of recovery can often be a prolonged, dismal one that is fraught with dangers and one which very possibly could end in failure – especially if you take on the challenge without the necessary tools required to complete the ascent and without the essential whole-heartedness and gritty determination needed to have a chance of succeeding in the first place.

Those initial feelings that I reckon gave *me* the will and strength to complete the challenge were ones of complete and utter disillusionment and disgust at myself for having fallen so helplessly and deeply into the snake-filled ravine of gambling addiction. These days, of I ever get even the slightest urge to have a punt, or if anyone in my social circles even suggests a trip to the casino or races, I slam the door firmly shut on the idea, simply by delving back into those feelings of despair of yesteryear when I was at the height (or maybe that should read lowest depth) of my addiction. I reckon this little exercise ought to work for most people. Just beginning to recall those gut-wrenching feelings experienced after handing over silly sums of money to those bastard bookies/casinos should, in theory, be sufficient to nip the possibility of a relapse in the bud (I'm assuming here some initial attempt has been made to quit the habit). But just as important is to vividly recall the very false highs that one experiences as a result of a hefty win. In fact, realizing and recalling these false feelings of triumph and elation are possibly even more crucial in a person's battle to quit than remembering the agony of those huge losses. A casino or bookie is more than happy to pay out to a 'winning' punter, as he knows that the poor wretch is oh so likely to give back these winnings in the future – **with interest.** That's why the "house always wins", as the saying goes. That's why Stanley's, Grosvenor, Ladbrokes, Hills and the rest are all still (very, very profitably) standing, and why so many gullible punters have been brought to their knees.

You really do have to remind yourself how sly and ruthless these gambling organisations really are, and you have to ask yourself these very pertinent questions: Do I, poor little old me, really stand a cat's chance in hell of getting the better of these monsters? Do I want to continue to aid and abet such vermin in their quest to relieve the masses of as much of their hard earned cash as possible? Are there not worthier, far less stressful things I could be doing with my life aside from risking money on the turn of a card or on the performance of a horse, dog, football team or golfer?? I am hoping that the answers to these questions come to you as quickly and as unequivocally as they come to me these days. Just in case there is any doubt at all as to what the answers *should* be, I will sound them out as a resounding **no, no,** and **yes.**

I always like to have as simplistic a take as possible on issues like this. Here's one of them; we are all only here, on this planet, once. We lead short lives, lives which unfortunately are usually replete with various struggles, difficulties and challenges along the way. Anybody in their right mind will acknowledge that life is *hard*. Therefore, I put this to you; why make things harder than they already are?? You only live the once, so for Pete's sake why not make your time here on this earth as rewarding and as comfortable as possible? OK, I am realistic enough to know that one can't *always* be comfortable. You might have to come out of your comfort zone regularly for various, obvious reasons. But that is totally fine, so long as you are helping yourself or somebody else in some sort of manner. What I *am* saying is that it is surely completely senseless and even foolhardy to get involved in anything bothersome and hassle-filled when it is absolutely unnecessary, morally dubious and completely of no help to anyone aside from those aforementioned daylight robbers who run the industry. I sincerely hope I am sounding convincing enough.

What disguises the problem, to the extent that it is all too shrouded in the confused (and that is putting it mildly) times I believe we are currently living through, is the mentality of modern, western society toward the issue of gambling. Not only is its destructive presence tolerated, it is positively exalted. For crying out loud, the queen herself, a person whom millions around the world are meant to look up to and hold in the highest regard, is an ardent racing fan and even attends long instituted royal meetings such as Ascot. She is even reputed to be most fond of a punt on the races herself, and apparently has a long standing debt yet to be settled with William Hills (oh ok, yes, I made that bit up. But it would be highly amusing if it was true, wouldn't it?!). On a more serious note, though, there can be no figure in this country, that said perhaps even in some other countries the world over, who possesses such a grand responsibility to set an outstanding example, than Her Majesty The Queen. Just imagine the uproar if she was caught with her feet up in the gardens of one of her palaces smoking a great big joint, then a few minutes later rolling around suffering from an uncontrollable fit of the giggles because she was so 'stoned'. Of course, this would never actually happen, because even if our dear old Queen was ever tempted to try out the old 'wacky baccy', I very much doubt her aides would be willing to go out and purchase any of the stuff from the local dealer!

Everybody *does* know, on the other hand, of her Majesty's fondness for a punt – but I don't ever recall hearing of any sort of disapproval of this habit of hers. I don't believe that the comparison of this vice with the unimaginable event of her dabbling in drug abuse is particularly over the top. In fact, many will agree that gambling *is* a drug to many people. But it appears to be quite accepted that our much loved monarch has a strong penchant for a punt in her leisure time, and that there is little wrong with this. To my mind it's as though she's saying to her loyal subjects, " never mind me while I fritter away some of my spare cash, it's only a harmless bit of fun, and the races *are* a most wonderful part of our British heritage, aren't they?"

Aye, Your Majesty, there's nowt wrong with a bit of a punt here and there. And never mind the fact that this 'fun' little habit can take a most horrible grip of a person and lead to a wasted life of misery and ruin in many cases. Never mind that. The authorities that be, the Queen herself and the government right down to our local councils, cannot be totally oblivious to a growing problem. The truth of the matter is that these people have no desire at all to actually *do* anything about the many who fall prey to the gambling bug. After all, the industry is another huge, money-making cog in the economy, and they wouldn't want to interfere with that now, would they? In fact, the establishment goes out of its way to commend those who have 'made it' by milking extortionate sums of money out of the general public. The boss of Stanley Leisure, a gambling organisation which is in the Premier League of bookmakers in this country and which owns several very sizeable casinos nationwide, has even been 'honoured' with a knighthood!!

I think this beggars belief. What kind of message is being sent out here? I bet Robin Hood would be turning in his grave if he heard of this; a man being granted the highest possible accolade for having robbed from the poor to make himself, and all his executive cronies, stupendously rich!

If you constantly remind yourself how much misery is wrought and how unfair and corrupt the whole industry is, this must surely act as a very tempting incentive to annihilate any problematic gambling habit and to rid yourself of it for good. If the Queen wants to spend her spare time gambling on the horses (and who knows what else), while those who run the country's gambling establishments, however large or small, are content to rob people of their resources to fill their own coffers, then so be it. Realistically speaking, there is absolutely bugger all people like you and I can do about it. What we can do, though, is resolve not to be a part of the sordid industry, save lots of money for ourselves and do whatever we can to help people we come across who might be getting involved more than is healthily advisable. My old pal Stuart (who, of course, was largely responsible for getting yours truly hooked in the first place, at a very impressionable young age) still needs help. Even though he is married with two nippers these days, he still persists in getting himself stuck up sh*t creek because he keeps getting involved in a habit he *knows* he cannot control. I caught up with him just a while back, and he reckons his most recent escapades nearly cost him his marriage. He had to come clean in the end and tell her everything, not just explaining why the bailiffs were round at their gaff for unpaid bills, but also how he had lost his job for nicking out of the company's funds. To say that she was unimpressed is an understatement of humungous proportions, and I imagine some choice words (and slaps to the face) were dished out in response! So when you hear of discord like that, it should put everyone, especially those who know they have addictive personalities in the first place, on high alert.

Obviously, I'm not making some bizarre statement that everyone who enjoys a punt is definitely headed for the scrap heap one day, but there is certainly the potential for some more than others to find themselves doing some very regrettable and senseless things to continue to fund a gambling habit that has taken a vice-like hold. And we all know who we are. In addition to the more likely candidates, I believe those of a more steady make up should also never become too complacent. As any mature person knows, life can throw up many situations that can lead to folk becoming reliant on any number of bad habits. Just don't let gambling be another one – no matter how hard it may seem at first to give up. It really is a case of mind prevailing over matter.

FINANCES IN A DEVILISH STATE

After over a dozen years of an unhealthy fixation with gambling, with the last four of those representing an almost manic spell of over-size punting, the state of your finances is not going to end up looking a pretty sight. Short of actually stealing, I went to some very silly lengths to get my hands on a lump sum of cash that would feed my habit for a few more months, or even weeks sometimes depending on how bad a patch I was going through and how much I had decided to lump on per bet at the time. My pal Stuart, who as I said actually took it upon himself to rob from the company coffers so he could chuck some more dosh at those lovely bookmakers, reckons the trouble I have found myself in is "nothing" compared to the stuff he has had to endure, what with bailiffs turning up at his gaff to reclaim debts, and his wife being the one who answered the door to deal with them, all the while totally baffled as to how her husband had got them into this mess. Plus he reckons the company he was working for was very lenient toward him after they discovered he had been nicking from them. He says he went through a terrible time wondering what the consequences of his actions might have led to.

This is all true - to a point - as I never went quite to the lengths my old pal did to acquire gambling funds. But I know him well enough after all these years, and I know him not to be the worrier that I certainly am. He definitely has more the attitude of 'sh*t happens and you just deal with it somehow'. I, however, do tend to get my knickers into more of a twist, and I do not look back fondly on all those sleepless nights I went through as a direct result of having blown a grand or two on the races that day. Of someone else's money. Money that I knew I would certainly struggle to pay back, or even pay back at all. I'm talking about borrowed money like bank loans and credit cards, and even ten grand's worth of car finance, a debt I took upon myself when possibly at the height of my profligacy. They soon got their car back, a swanky (at least judging by the de luxe interior) looking Peugeot 406 Exec. model if I remember right. I recall one particularly bad day at the races which resulted in me chucking their car back at them, as I finally realised how badly they had ripped me off and how I needed to implement some very drastic cost cutting measures!

I was, as usual, trying my best to stick to my firmly held belief that one big bet a day was more than enough, and win, lose, or draw (i.e. have an each-way bet come placed) it was only right and proper to walk straight out of that shop and get on with doing something else for the rest of the day. This, I always thought, was a sensible course of action for a few reasons. First up, if the bet was a losing one, it would stop me 'chasing' and putting down what could be several more excessive, ill-advised bets in an often vain attempt to recoup the losses from the initial failure. Secondly, it would prevent the nervous tension that I always found quite overwhelming when stuck in the bookies (or in front of teletext) all afternoon, placing bet after bet hoping the animal I had backed (or even the jockeys, in many instances) could be arsed running a half decent race and giving us tired old punters a run for our money. Thirdly, sticking to just one bet a day, whatever the outcome of the race, gave you a better chance of limiting your losses, or even sometimes showing a profit, in the long run. This was because, as I and many of my esteemed co-gamblers believed, your judgement would not become clouded for the following races if you did call it quits for the day after the one punt. You see, if my selection had run a stinker, it would just have the knack of knocking me off balance enough to make a silly selection in the next race. And if I started off with a sizeable win, and gave me a delusion of invincibility and that it was 'my day', and that whatever I backed would probably fly home by six lengths for a facile success.

Despite, on the face of it, all this pretty measured reasoning, I would fall off the wagon regularly and endure a reckless, wild afternoon of punting that would blow yet another irreparable hole into any of my various credit cards or bank loans. Or miss yet another month's repayment on my car finance. My good mate Darkie, who of course was often present during the course of these destructive afternoon punting sessions, was always sure to be forthcoming with words of reassurance when he could see I had done my bollocks in yet again.

"Don't worry about it, my son, none of them bastards will miss the money. They've got plenty, haven't they? And there's f*ck all they can do about it anyway, it's not like you've got a house to lose or anything. ."

This was true, as I had always flitted back and forth between rented bed-sits and my folks' house over the years, and had never even thought about going all steady and investing in a property. That would be far too sensible for me. What Darkie *did* neglect to tell me was that every time I neglected a credit card, bank loan, car finance or even mobile phone payment, my status with those people, who kept records of everyone's credit history, was suffering even more of a battering! Maybe he assumed I knew all this stuff as a matter of course, or maybe he was pleased to see someone else getting in as much sh*t as he had managed to get himself into over the years, including the massive bad debts he had managed to accrue when his investments in the stock market, all with borrowed money, evaporated following a mini-crash somewhere around the turn of the Millenium.

The result is that neither Darkie nor I can now get a pack of *fags* on tick, let alone a car or property! In a weird kind of way, you just have to laugh about it. If you don't, you'll only cry, as the saying goes. Although, I suppose, we wouldn't be laughing if we did desperately require a loan for something or other, but obviously I hope it never does come to that. Having gone through many an afternoon of crushing losses, Darkie and I would usually sit down over a pint or six and work out where our next batch of funds could come from. He would come up with some very dodgy sounding 'schemes', having consulted his even dodgier 'business' partners, and was usually very keen to get yours truly involved, at least when my credit status was half intact anyway. Luckily, despite the promise of some very sizeable returns, I never got involved with any of his monkey business. I didn't particularly trust him or any of his proposed ventures, especially when he went about running me through what was roughly involved. I like to think I am ok at sniffing out a stinking rat these days; I have been ripped of a couple of times before by so called 'mates', so I can see these things coming from quite a distance off.

Besides which, I am not at all comfortable about going out of my way to get into debt with big organisations, even if it is a fact that they wouldn't miss the money and that they don't turn over hundreds of millions a year by generally being sympathetic and lenient with people (viz extortionate penalty charges and the like).

But the destructive influence of Darkie is no excuse. Getting into thousands of pounds of debt with various people because of a gambling disease is one thing, but there comes a time when you have to admit defeat and consider it all one very big, costly mistake, which I believe in many cases is a result of the huge pull of our gambling culture itself, as much as it the fault of those who get themselves into trouble from it. But then going out to basically steal when you find you have scraped the bottom of your resources is just going that extra step too far. Gambling, however, somehow possesses this extraordinary pull to get people to do things they would never normally give the time of day. You always have to remember the root cause before judging peoples' actions and reactions, so I do always bring this to mind when I hear of my ex-gambling mates' latest dubious escapades to find more gambling reserves.

I guess I am lucky that I realised I had a problem with gambling before I got involved in anything *too* daft to get my hands on more money. I dread to think it could ever have got to that stage, but you do never really know in this life. As it happens, I do have several debts that I doubt I will ever be able to get rid of. This includes that wretched car I got on finance, which I purchased in the midst of a massive rush of blood to the head after a good day at 'the office', and which got given back after one of those awful afternoons where I chased losses, probably doubling up on my stakes all the while, and ended up doing in absurd bundles of cash.

A big, burly fella of bouncer-ish appearance turned up to take the big lump of metal away, and he could see the agitated state I was in having not too long ago chucked away a small fortune. Not that he exactly knew that. But I think he could tell I was not a happy camper that afternoon, judging by the relatively understanding and even gentle approach he took when relieving me of the '406'. He said I had to suggest a monthly sum I could commit to paying back the finance company, to pay off the balance that would be owing once they had confirmed what they would be deducting as the car's value. I immediately, and quite genuinely, started panicking about how I would be able to afford anything whatsoever; that I was in a terrible position and I had a load of other creditors on my back, all hassling me for payment. I told him that my 'business' affairs had taken a horrible turn for the worst, and that I would be subsisting on hand-outs for the foreseeable future. The kind man seemed sympathetic to my grovelling and muttered something about scribbling down "any old amount" on the sheet that I had to sign.

"Don't worry about it, just tell 'em you can do a few quid a month, just as a gesture. Should we call it twenty quid a month? That ok?"

I told him I really was up the old sh*t creek without a paddle and that I could only agree to a tenner – if they were lucky. He again told me not to worry too much about the whole thing, asked if I was sure I had salvaged everything of any worth whatsoever from the car, took the keys off me, and that was that. Another episode over and done with – and the end of another saga started and finished by my stupid, over the top gambling.

I turned up at the local that night, as usual determined to numb my mind - with the considerable aid of a few hours' alcohol intake- of the day's events. Being a balmy summer's night, all the lads were sat outside enjoying their lager, when I turned up in a cab. Just as they all wondered how the hell a scruffy rogue such as I could afford a swish motor in the first place, the inquisition began as to why I had got rid of it after merely a few months. I just fobbed them off with some mutterings about how I couldn't be bothered finding the repayments each month, and how I didn't really need the damn thing in the first place! Which was quite probably true, as I was, on average, sober enough only a couple of times a week to drive it anywhere. And when it did go anywhere, it was usually to that pub where it got ditched and forgotten about while I either celebrated a nice win (buying drinks for virtually everyone in sight) or drowned out the sorrows of a loss. Of course the losses almost always amounted to much more than the wins – plus the beer/vodka expenses thrown in. All in a day's work, eh?

To be quite frank, I have accrued such debts that I have fobbed off most of my creditors. It's certainly wrong, but I do owe that much that it really doesn't bear thinking about too much. I must have racked up over £40,000 worth of debt, but I can't even muster the courage nor inclination to go through the process of totting it up, as the memories of all those reckless times are spectres I want to bury forever. Yes, I am no longer credit worthy. But what am I to give these creditors? My backside? My pet chinchilla?

Never mind though. As Dodgy Darkie always so succinctly puts it, the buggers won't miss it too much!

THE FINAL SLAYING OF THE DEVIL

Having tossed away so much money and valuable time, and having really struggled to properly convince myself that I had a problem that needed urgent and immediate attention, there came a pivotal point where a decided enough really was enough. There were the times I had succeeded in giving it up for a while at a time, maybe a few weeks here and there where I managed to steer clear of gambling. You could, I guess, compare it in a way to an alcoholic who had managed to go without a drink for a period of time, but for one reason or another came to fall off the wagon again, once he'd succumbed to the temptation of the demon drink. And I reckon people who have a gambling sickness are similar to alcoholics in that they only need to have a small taste of their nemesis, before it leads to a prolonged and unhealthy bender that undoes all the hard and well intentioned effort that led to a temporary, albeit shaky reprieve. It happened to me many times, probably on over a dozen occasions. After letting loose and going on an all-afternoon punting 'bender', my head would be spinning trying to calculate the extent of the damage incurred. I would come out of the bookies proverbially spitting blood, almost wanting to scream out loud in the street in frustration and raw anger. How could I have been so daft as to have fallen into the same trap once again? I knew where the trap was, how painful it was and how long it took for the wounds to heal. So why the hell keep going back for more? It felt something like self-pugilism.

Yes, I knew then as well as I know now that the key is to keep busy doing something else; to constantly take your mind off gambling by immersing yourself in a different outlet, whether it be with respect to your working or leisure life. I have never personally been the type that lives to work, as opposed to those who merely see their work as a necessary tool to get by and that life is there to be enjoyed to the maximum. Having read the most part of this book, I am certain that, by now, you readers have realised that I definitely belong to the latter group! As someone once said to me – "we're here for a good time not for a long time, aren't we Mike!" I found that particularly amusing and it rang quite true in my view. Anyway, what I am trying to get at here is that I am never going to be so obsessed or immersed in any work that I am always, inevitably going to have a welcome distraction that prevents me getting caught up in my old my bad habit. Likewise, I personally don't have any leisure pursuits that would act as an equally potent distraction. So for me, I have just had to come to my own conclusion that gambling is a rancid, destructive force that is only ever going to hamper my quality of life as opposed to enhancing it. So what on earth is the point?

After those several aborted, failed attempts to finally quit I finally managed the big breakthrough. I can't explain exactly what, but something hit me, something that finally made me wake up to the fact that I **had** to quit, or else I would just suffer for the rest of my life from this addiction. I think things kind of reached a crescendo, as they sometimes have to, before I seriously took it upon myself to jack it all in. I think it's that feeling of everything spiralling out of control that really hits your inner guts and makes you stop. Well I hope it makes most people who suffer this damnable feeling stop, or at least give the idea some serious thought.

I have actually just recently finished off reading Paul Gascoigne's autobiography, and as most people will know, that guy has been through some really awful times. The problem he developed with alcohol was, in more or less these words, "more a result of what I've been through rather than the cause of the problems themselves." I believe that, in so many cases, gambling is, similarly, a so-called escape for many people from their problems, rather than the instigator itself. So we all really do have to recognize this before trying to move forward and doing something about it. Gazza also recognized that it wasn't until everything, his alcoholism included, came to a head, that he sought serious help to give up. He also mentioned a couple of times how the booze started to catch up on him as he got into his thirties, in both a physical and mental sense – he realised how the combination of boozing and playing professional football at the top level could simply no longer go hand in hand.

The thing with gambling that I found was that it began to catch up with me mentally, that every time I went on a punting 'bender' and gave over all my winnings, or even worse did in a load of cash that I hadn't even won in the first place, I began to feel more and more idiotic and helpless each time – feelings that would sometimes even touch on humiliation. In that sense it was, I suppose, a good thing that I was growing so fed up and weary with my excesses. I was getting tired of pressing my self-destruct button and realised it was time to move on. Obviously, I would love to say to everyone who has a problem - and I know there are many people with worse problems than I've had to contend with - that the best and only way to give up is to decide to stop, get some help from someone or somewhere, and with a click of the fingers the whole thing has dissolved into nothing. But, unfortunately, I get the impression the reality is that those with an addictive nature often have to hit rock bottom before rising to the surface once more. Then again, everyone has their own version of what rock bottom actually is – does it amount to losing absolutely everything until you are actually in the gutter? For some the answer to that might be yes. For me, it was when I realised that gambling had virtually taken over my life that things had to change. Everything depended on whether I was on a winning streak or not; my mood, my relationship with my family, my social life, my drinking habits, whether I could go on holiday with the lads or not, and, of course, how well I slept at night. That's exactly how much it affected things. Scary when I look back now.

One of the tactics I did employ when finally managing to put a lid on all of this was to distance myself from people around me who were still very much into their gambling. I know it sounds feeble and even cowardly to even hint that others were very much responsible for me getting into a gambling habit in the first place, and for doing absolutely nothing to halt my slide into the mess that followed when the habit escalated to such a degree. But the truth is that in my adult life I always seem to have been surrounded by serpentine individuals who have tried to tempt me to eat that forbidden fruit. Maybe one of the down sides to having grown up in quite an affluent neighbourhood is that my pals always seemed to have a reserve of cash to burn. Not always such a lot, but always something. Even before many entered into full time employment, they seemed to have sugar daddies of sorts who would wilfully finance their wild sorties, even if just to get them out of the house for a bit. I really do wonder what they honestly thought their lovely offspring would do with these funds in their ample spare time – buy a pint or two then grab a kebab on the way home? Nope. Not with these lot. Drugs and gambling was the order of the day, and I got sucked in, as I have already chronicled, in a big way.

Then Darkie came along, and, lacking a gambling partner at the time, was more than pleased to welcome me on board to throw good money overboard and into the waters with him. He knew how hooked I had become, but never even so much as gave me a nudge in the direction away from the bookmakers and casinos of Manchester. I still don't hold this against him; I ought to have been much wiser to what I was getting myself into and how deep into the crap I was sinking. But I have distanced myself from him, his dodgy money making schemes and his general influence. Sometimes you really don't realise just how much of an influence those you mix with can be. I like to think I have never wittingly persuaded anyone into getting involved in bad habits, whether I was going through my own phases of various excesses or not. As I have stated, apart from all the gambling, I have had my problems with substance abuse as well – mainly drink and 'soft' drugs (although I vehemently contest whether there *is* such a thing as a soft drug or not). Those however are *my* choices and *my* problems and it is not up to *me* to get others into similar bad habits. But other people seem to have had no problem dragging me into *their* murky worlds, then dropping me like a stone once they decided they

had had enough, thank you very much. With friends like these
. . . I'm sure you know how the rest of that saying goes.

There's no room for regrets or bitterness, though. What's
done is done, and the mess is slowly being cleaned up. Just as I
have been writing this, I was interrupted by a phone call – an
old creditor trying to get money out of me. . a mobile phone
bill for a few hundred quid that I managed to rack up. These
kind of things just serve as a reminder of my not-so-glorious
past, but there's not a lot that can be done. Without skirting
any preliminaries, the woman requested payment 'in full', there
and then over the phone, and then started going on about legal
proceedings and bailiffs, and all that kind of b*ll*cks, if I didn't
pay. I calmly responded that I was in a sh*te situation (not
using those precise words, of course), and that I was living on
hand-outs for the while. And I also told her that I wasn't very
well, either, which is true . . I regularly suffer panic attacks and
some quite severe depression, a kind of post-traumatic stress
perhaps. I know a lot of people move effortlessly on from bad
experiences in their life, but I am perhaps not as tough as those
such types – all the bad memories of drugs, bad decisions, worse
jobs and even worse relationships regularly come back to haunt
my admittedly fragile mind. . and, naturally, all those years of
gambling are still etched in the rich if not very aesthetically
pleasing tapestry of my life. I may have stopped the gambling
monster in its once rampant tracks, and for that matter killed
off and buried some other very nasty habits. But I will still go

out drinking, thankfully not too heavily, on the strength of my past glorious failures.

You might think I am laying out something of a sob story here, and yes, I do realise how many people there are on our planet who are far, far worse off than I. But unfortunately, that is the way I have winded up feeling. And all that damned gambling has certainly left some very noticeable chinks in my armour. I hope that everyone who has joined me on this written journey of my life so far, especially gambling life, can see just how damaging this scourge has been for me, how anybody of any age, creed or background is not immune from the bug and how potentially dangerous it is for our future generations, what with all the technology we now have access to and how the gambling powers that be are exploiting this to milk more and more vulnerable folk.. I can only hope that I have in some way helped a few people out there, especially those who are of an addictive psyche and have had real trouble, to date, doing anything about their problem. I hope you have been able to identify with my experiences and feelings expressed, and I sincerely hope I have given some sort of wake-up call to those who blindly carry on tossing money in the direction of those greedy people, money that they can ill afford to lose if they are honest with themselves. Even if I've only actually succeeded in helping a handful of people I will feel satisfied that I have bothered to write all this stuff. I know I'm no professional, like some sort of counsellor or something, but I hope that just by recounting my own experiences and battles I will have helped convince some gambling addicts to seriously consider kicking it all in, and to kick it all in *for good*. And even if you're reading this and don't suffer a particularly bad gambling habit, I hope I have succeeded in giving stern warning as to what can happen if you're not very, very watchful. We are all only human.

Ta for reading, and good luck to you all. Not at the bookies or gaming tables, of course. But on *not* going there to play at all. Remember. . there are lots of better things to do with your time!

www.ingramcontent.com/pod-product-compliance
Lightning Source LLC
Chambersburg PA
CBHW031246280526
45784CB00004B/1743